Invited by Christ

Preparing for First Reconciliation and First Eucharist

Pflaum
SACRAMENTAL PREPARATION

Imprimatur
+Most Reverend Robert J. McManus, S.T.D.
Bishop of Worcester
January 2, 2023

English Edition
Publisher: David M. Dziena
Project Editor: Heidi Witte
Project Designer: Jennifer Poferl

Original Publication in France
Concept: Nord. Compo

© Éditions CRER-Bayard - March 2016
19, rue de la Saillerie - CS 10002
49184 Saint-Barthélemy-d'Anjou Cedex
www.editions.crer-bayard.fr
Registered in France: March 2016
Printed in France: January 2016

Acknowledgments
Scripture texts in this work are taken from the *New American Bible*, revised edition © 2010, 1991, 1986, 1970 Confraternity of Christian Doctrine, Washington, D.C. and are used by permission of the copyright owner. All Rights Reserved. No part of the *New American Bible* may be reproduced in any form without permission in writing from the copyright owner.

Excerpts from the English translation of the *Catechism of the Catholic Church* for use in the United States of America Copyright © 1994, United States Catholic Conference, Inc.— Libreria Editrice Vaticana. Used with Permission. English translation of the *Catechism of the Catholic Church*: Modifications from the Editio Typica copyright © 1997, United States Conference of Catholic Bishops—Libreria Editrice Vaticana.

Excerpts from the English translation of *The Roman Missal* © 2010, International Commission on English in the Liturgy Corporation, (ICEL); the English translation of *The Order of Penance* © 2019, ICEL. All rights reserved.

English translation of the Glory Be to the Father and Lord's Prayer by the International Consultation on English Texts (ICET).

Photos: pages 5, 9, 16, 21, 32, 49, 54: ©John Roman/Thinkstock; pages 5, 49: ©VaticanMedia-Foto/CPP/CIRIC; page 9 (left): ©GuillaumeProject; pages 10 (top), 19, 45 (center), 51, 52: ©SDC Toulouse; page 10 (center): ©Jean Matthieu Gautier/CIRIC; page 10 (bottom): ©Guillaume Poli/CIRIC; page 17: ©Killmayer; pages 18 (top), 27, 43, 48, 74 (center, right): ©Corinne Simon/CIRIC; page 18 (bottom): ©Roman Catholic Archdiocese of Boston, photo by George Martel: BCDS (CC BY-ND 2.0) via Flickr.com; page 28: ©Pololia/stock.adobe.com; page 30 (left): ©Adam Ján Figel'/stock.adobe.com; page 30 (top right): ©Marcel Crozet/CIRIC; pages 30 (bottom right), 72 (right), 74 (left): ©2016 Robert Carlin Photography Inc.; page 38: ©William Alix/CIRIC; page 39: ©Alain Pinoges/CIRIC; page 42: ©Herney Gómez/pixabay.com; page 45 (top left, bottom left): ©Kalmukanin/Thinkstock; page 45 (center left): ©Halfpoint/Thinkstock; page 45 (top right): ©Oliver Meadows/Thinkstock; page 45 (center right): ©C12/Thinkstock; page 45 (bottom right): ©Zatletic/stock.adobe.com; page 46: ©Jean Christophe Verhaegen/CIRIC; page 47: © Michael Bunel/CIRIC; page 52 (center, left): ©Albert; page 60: ©Wojtek Buss/CIRIC; page 68: © Sewcream/stock.adobe.com; page 69: ©aceshot/stock.adobe.com; page 69: ©Dorothée Quennesson/pixabay.com; pages 72 (left), 73 (left); ©Steve Check; page 73 (right): ©EDA; page 75 (left): ©Kasia Strek/CIRIC; page 75 (center): ©Cyril Badet/CIRIC, ©Lukasz Pajor/stock.adobe.com: page 75 (right): pages 7 (right), 21 (lower half), 33: All illustrations by Stephan Laplanche, except ©Freepik; pages 20, 36, 37 (right), 40-41 ©Gommedesbois.

Pflaum Publishing Group
3055 Kettering Blvd.
Dayton, OH 45439
800-543-4383
pflaum.com

ISBN 978-1-947358-65-2
Printed in the USA.

Contents

Let's take the First Communion Bus together!

STEP 5
Invited to the Banquet
SECOND PARENT MEETING
STEP 6
At the Lord's Table:
Celebration of First Eucharist
STEP 7
Entering into the Mysteries
HI, MY NAME IS SARAH.
HI, I'M BENJAMIN.
WHAT'S YOUR NAME?

First Communion Bus
STEP 1
Called
by God

From the Bible

THE CALL OF SAMUEL

1 Samuel 3:1-10, 19-21

When the young Samuel was the servant of the LORD under Eli, the word of the LORD was rare and visions weren't common. One day, Eli was asleep in his usual place. His eyes had lately grown so weak that he could not see. The lamp of God was not yet extinguished, and Samuel was sleeping in the temple of the LORD where the ark of God was. The LORD called to Samuel, who answered, "Here I am." He ran to Eli and said, **"Here I am. You called me."** "I did not call you," Eli answered. "Go back to sleep." So he went back to sleepage

Again the LORD called Samuel, who rose and went to Eli. "Here I am," he said. "You called me." But he answered, "I did not call you, my son. Go back to sleep." Samuel did not yet recognize the LORD, since **the word of the LORD had not yet been revealed to him.**

The LORD called Samuel again, for the third time. Getting up and going to Eli, he said, "Here I am. You called me." Then Eli understood that the LORD was calling the boy. So he said to Samuel, "Go to sleep, and if you are called, reply, 'Speak, LORD, for your servant is listening.'" When Samuel went to sleep in his place, the LORD came and stood there, calling out as before: "Samuel, Samuel!" Samuel answered, **"Speak, for your servant is listening."**

Samuel grew up, and the LORD was with him and made everything that Samuel said come true. And all of Israel from Dan to Beer-sheba came to know that Samuel was a trustworthy prophet of the LORD. The LORD continued to appear at Shiloh, revealing himself to Samuel at Shiloh **through his word.** Samuel's word spread throughout Israel.

Look at the comic strip and retell the story of Samuel using your own words.

Eli helped Samuel recognize God's call. Who has helped you learn about Jesus?

God Calls You!

You have been called by God since your **Baptism**! The Sacrament of Baptism is the first step of your journey toward First Eucharist. Every baptized Catholic is called and chosen by Christ to live as a child of God. Baptism washes away our Original Sin—the sin we are born with that separates us from God. In Baptism, we receive the gift of sanctifying grace, which gives us new life in Christ and makes us members of the Church family.

Making the **Sign of the Cross** with holy water reminds us of our Baptism and God's love for us!

Catholic Faith Word

BAPTISM– The sacrament that makes us children of God and members of God's family, the Church.

PRAYER

You see me, Lord, and you know me!
You know my every move.
You are deep in my heart.
From morning to evening
you accompany me.
Even before I speak, you know what I'm going to say. Amen.

Adapted from Psalm 139:1-4

CATECHISM Q&A

Q What happens when someone is baptized?

A Baptism takes away Original Sin. It allows us to share in the divine life of the Trinity through sanctifying grace, which makes us members of Christ and the Church. It gives us a share in the priesthood of Christ and unity with all Christians. We receive the theological virtues and the gifts of the Holy Spirit. A baptized person belongs forever to Christ (1262—1274, 1279-1280).

WITH MY FAMILY

Discuss

Talk with your child about why he or she wants to prepare for the Sacrament of the Eucharist. Write down your child's response on a piece of paper, and place it somewhere where your child can see it daily.

STEP 2
One Body in Christ

★ Using the Word Bank, choose several words that can help us as we travel together on this First Communion journey. Write them on your backpack; then decorate it.

Word Bank:

- ☐ PATIENCE
- ☐ ANGER
- ☐ TEAMWORK
- ☐ DISRESPECT
- ☐ FAITHFULNESS
- ☐ LISTENING
- ☐ COMPETITION
- ☐ COOPERATION
- ☐ SHARING

From the Bible

JESUS MEETS BARTIMAEUS

Mark 10:46-52

And as Jesus was leaving Jericho with his disciples and a large crowd, Bartimaeus, a blind man and the son of Timaeus, sat by the roadside begging. On hearing that it was Jesus of Nazareth, he began to cry out and say, **"Jesus, son of David, have pity on me."** And many scolded him, telling him to be silent. But he kept calling out all the more, "Son of David, have pity on me."

Jesus stopped and said, "Call him." So they called the blind man, saying to him, "Take courage; **get up, he is calling you."**

He threw aside his cloak, sprang up, and came to Jesus. Jesus said to him in reply, **"What do you want me to do for you?"** The blind man replied to him, "Master, I want to see."

Jesus told him, "Go your way; your faith has saved you." Immediately **he received his sight and followed Jesus** on the road.

Jesus asks each of us the question above. Create a short, personal prayer to Jesus, asking him to help you with something challenging in your life.

PRAYER

When the people heard you had arrived in Jericho, they gathered.

Today we have heard you and we have come, too. Thank you, Lord, for your invitation.

Guided by the crowd, Bartimaeus approached. With our parents and the members of our parish community, we come together as your Church family. For those who are here with us, thank you, Lord.

Bartimaeus' eyes were opened and he was happy. He followed you. Guided by your Cross, we walk toward you. We thank you, Lord, for your love and for our lives. Amen.

YOU'RE INVITED TO THE EUCHARISTIC CELEBRATION!

The Church is not just a building. The **Church** is the Body of Christ gathered in the name of Jesus, who is the head of the body. Together, the People of God answer the call of the Lord, gathering at **Mass** each Sunday to celebrate the Risen Christ. We come to give thanks for the gift of the Eucharist, which is the center of the Church's life.

The Order of Mass

Introductory Rites

- **ENTRANCE PROCESSION:** As everyone sings the gathering song, the altar servers carry the cross toward the altar, and the celebrant—a priest or bishop—follows.
- **SIGN OF THE CROSS AND GREETING:** At the altar, the celebrant welcomes us in the name of the Father, and of the Son, and of the Holy Spirit, and we make the Sign of the Cross.
- **PENITENTIAL ACT:** We recognize that we are sinners and that we need Jesus to save us. We say, "Lord, have mercy."
- **GLORIA:** Because Jesus offers us forgiveness, we joyfully praise God by singing this hymn.
- **COLLECT:** The priest or bishop concludes with an opening prayer, called the Collect.

Catholic Faith Words

MASS–The Catholic Church's central act of public worship.

CHURCH–The People of God gathered in the name of Jesus Christ.

EUCHARIST–The sacrament in which we receive Jesus' Body and Blood to nourish us and help us to become more like him.

WORD SEARCH

Find these words hidden in the grid:

- FRIEND • LOVE • TOGETHER • COMMUNITY • JOY
- PLAY • JUSTICE • THANKS • PEACE • FORGIVE • SHARE
- PRAYER • MEALS • REST • SERVICE

M	E	A	L	S	B	X	T	C	S
F	L	P	U	P	J	Z	O	O	H
F	T	R	E	L	O	Z	G	M	A
O	H	E	S	A	Y	U	E	M	R
R	A	Y	E	Y	C	D	T	U	E
G	N	A	R	R	N	E	H	N	L
I	K	R	V	E	E	W	E	I	O
V	S	P	I	D	S	S	R	T	V
E	W	R	C	M	Y	R	T	Y	E
Q	F	Z	E	C	I	T	S	U	J

Use the highlighted letters to form a word that reminds us of the reason for our trip this year. Write the word below.

CATECHISM Q&A

Q What is the meaning of the Eucharist in the life of the Church?

A The Eucharist is the source and summit of all Christian life: the highest form of worshipage The Eucharist makes us one with Christ while also uniting us with the People of God (the Church). In the Eucharistic celebration, we receive a taste of what eternal life will be like (1324-1327, 1407).

WITH MY FAMILY Discuss

With your child, identify words from the list that express what he or she is experiencing while preparing to receive the Eucharist. Next, select the words that describe what you share as a family. Give some specific examples to explain the words you have chosen. Then, select one or two that you would like to focus on in your family life. Ask the Holy Spirit for the strength to keep this promise.

STEP 3

Living in God's Covenant

A	C	D	E	F	G	H	I	N	O	P	R	S	T	V
🍩	🎉	🏀	🎻	🎒	🙂	🌺	☘️	⛅	✏️	🌲	🎤	🌎	🐌	🐞

★ Decode the message to continue our journey on the First Communion bus.

Walk to the traffic circle of 🎒 🎤 ☘️ 🎻 ⛅ 🏀 🌎 🌺 ☘️ 🌲

Take the second right onto the road of 🌲 🍩 🐌 ☘️ 🎻 ⛅ 🎉 🎻

Then take a left, toward the path of 🎒 ✏️ 🎤 🙂 ☘️ 🐞 🎻 ⛅ 🎻 🌎 🌎

Stop for a moment at the stoplight of 🌎 🌺 🍩 🎤 ☘️ ⛅ 🙂

Go in the direction of the Avenue of the 🎉 ✏️ 🐞 🎻 ⛅ 🍩 ⛅ 🐌

"See, I am now establishing my **covenant** with you and your descendants after you…" (Genesis 9:9)

Catholic Faith Word

COVENANT—A commitment or agreement of faith and love between God and his people.

Throughout history, God renewed his covenant by choosing special helpers from the people of Israel to proclaim His Word.

God's Covenant with His People

Using your Bible, look up these Scripture verses. Fill in the missing words.

God Speaks to Noah

I set my ________ in the clouds to serve as a sign of the covenant between me and the earth (Genesis 9:13).

The Story of Abraham

On that day the LORD made a covenant with Abram, saying: To your descendants I give this ________ (Genesis 15:18).

Between you and me I will establish my ________, and I will give you many descendants (Genesis 17:2).

The Story of Moses

He proclaimed to you his covenant, which he commanded you to keep: the ten words, which he wrote on two ________ ________ (Deuteronomy 4:13).

Then he took the ________ and splashed it on the people, saying, "This is the blood of the covenant which the LORD has made with you according to all these words" (Exodus 24:8).

1800 BC

1270 BC

Important stories from the Book of Genesis

God speaks to Jeremiah

See, days are coming...when I will make a new covenant...I will place my law within them, and write it upon their ________ **(Jeremiah 31:31,33).**

The Letter to the Hebrews

May the God of peace, who brought up from the dead the great shepherd of the sheep by the blood of the ________ ________, Jesus our LORD, furnish you with all that is good, that you may do his will... through Jesus Christ, to whom be glory forever and ever. Amen **(Hebrews 13:20-21).**

Jesus

"This cup is the new covenant in my ________, which will be shed for you" **(Luke 22:20).**

PRAYER

[To be prayed in the style of the Examen]

Here I am, Lord;
with all my heart, I bless your name.
Thank you for everything you give us.

Praise be to you, Lord, you who are righteous and who defend the little ones.

Praise be to you, Lord, for the covenant you made with humanity: from Noah and then with the people of Israel to Abraham, Moses, and all prophets.

Praise be to you, Lord,
because you always trust us, even when we stray from you.
Guide us to you every moment of our lives.

Praise be to you, Lord, for Jesus, your Son, who shows us your great love.
Amen.

In Jesus, God offers us a new and eternal covenant. Sin can take us away from this promise of love. In prayer, we can come back to God. "Thank you," "forgive me," and "please" are good ways to start our prayers to our Lord. Using one of the words in the bubbles, write your own short prayer below.

THANK YOU

FORGIVE ME

PLEASE

....

....

....

....

....

....

....

....

....

Whoever loves me will keep my word, and my Father will love him, and we will come to him and make our home with him. John 14:23

THE PARABLE OF THE VINE AND THE BRANCHES

From the Bible

John 15:1-5

I am the true vine, and my Father is the vine grower. He takes away every branch in me that does not bear fruit, and every one that does, he prunes it so that it **bears more fruit.** You are already pruned because of the word that I spoke to you.

Remain in me, as I remain in you. Just as a branch cannot bear fruit on its own unless it remains on the vine, so neither can you unless you stay with me.

I am the vine, you are the branches. Whoever remains in me and I in him will bear much fruit, because without me you can do nothing.

Catholic Faith Word

WORD OF GOD–Another word for the Bible or Scripture.

What do the vine, the winegrower, and the branches represent?

JESUS IS THE VINE; WE ARE THE BRANCHES. THE BRANCHES ARE CONNECTED TO THE VINE AND ARE FED BY SAP FROM THE VINE. JESUS USES THIS IMAGE TO EXPLAIN THAT HE WANTS US TO STAY UNITED WITH HIM.

GOD PRUNES THE VINE SO THAT IT BEARS MORE FRUIT. WE CAN'T PRODUCE FRUIT ON OUR OWN. GOD TAKES CARE OF US BY GUIDING OUR WAY TO TRUE HAPPINESS.

THE **WORD OF GOD** CONNECTS US TO CHRIST SO THAT WE CAN BEAR FRUIT. BY LISTENING AND KEEPING GOD'S WORD IN OUR HEARTS AND PUTTING IT INTO ACTION IN OUR LIVES, WE STAY UNITED TO HIM.

WE BEAR MUCH FRUIT: BY LOVING LIKE JESUS DID, WE BRING JOY AND HAPPINESS TO THOSE AROUND US.

AT CHURCH

LISTEN TO GOD'S WORD!

The Order of Mass

Liturgy of the Word

- **FIRST READING:** A lector, or reader, proclaims a passage from the Old Testament, which tells the history of God's first covenant with humanity.
- **RESPONSORIAL PSALM:** We sing prayers to God like God's Chosen People did long ago.
- **SECOND READING:** We listen to a passage from the New Testament. These readings tell us the story of the first Christians, who share with us their faith in the Risen Christ.
- **GOSPEL ACCLAMATION:** We stand and sing "Alleluia" (except during Lent, when a different acclamation is sung).
- **GOSPEL READING:** We stand and listen to a story about Jesus. Incense or candles surround the ambo, showing us that the Gospel is important. Christ is present in his Word and proclaims the Good News to us!
- **THE HOMILY:** The priest or deacon explains the day's readings. He shows how God is alive and active in the world today.
- **THE PROFESSION OF FAITH:** We stand and proclaim the Creed, a prayer that tells what we believe as a Church.
- **THE PRAYER OF THE FAITHFUL:** We pray for our needs and the needs of the Church, community, and world.

Catholic Faith Word

LITURGY OF THE WORD—One of the two main parts of the Mass, during which we hear God's Word from the Bible and reflect on what it means for our lives.

When it's time to listen to the **Gospel** ...

The priest or deacon says:

"The Lord be with you."

We respond:

"And with your Spirit."

The priest or deacon says:

"A reading from the holy Gospel according to...."

And we respond:

"Glory to you, O Lord."

The priest or deacon traces a cross on the page of the Book of the Gospels. We also trace a small cross on our foreheads, on our lips, and on our hearts.

Catholic Faith Word

GOSPELS–The first four books in the New Testament that tell the Good News of Jesus' life, Death, and Resurrrection.

[The Word] is something very near to you, in your mouth and in your heart... Deuteronomy 30:14

I welcome the Word of God

Tracing the Sign of the Cross on my forehead, I pray:

Lord, may your Word enlighten my mind so that I understand the message you have for me today.

Tracing the Sign of the Cross on my mouth, I pray:

Lord, open my lips so I can tell everyone about your love, and say to all those who seek you that your Word gives me life.

Tracing the Sign of the Cross on my heart, I pray:

Lord, fill my heart with joy and hope so that I may live with others in your love.

WITH MY FAMILY

Discuss

As a family, select a Gospel passage that you especially love. Have each family member take a turn reading the Gospel story you chose. Explain why you picked this passage and why it is important.

GOSPEL PASSAGE: ....

....

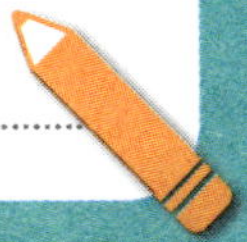

....

WHY OUR FAMILY PICKED THIS PASSAGE: ....

....

....

....

....

....

....

Pray

During the week, pray this prayer together.

Lord, may your Word enlighten me.

Lord, fill my heart with joy and hope every time I hear your Word.

Lord, open my lips so I can tell everyone about your love. Amen.

CATECHISM Q&A

Q What happens during the celebration of the Eucharist?

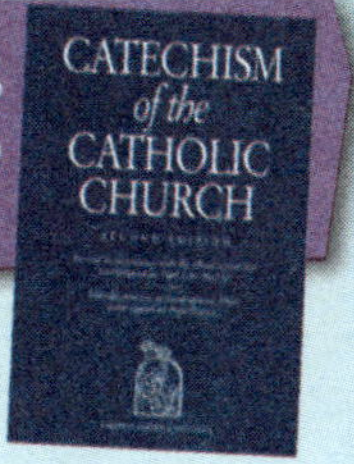

A The Eucharist unfolds in two great parts which together form one, single act of worshipage The Liturgy of the Word involves proclaiming and listening to the Word of God. The Liturgy of the Eucharist includes the presentation of the bread and wine, the Eucharistic prayer containing the words of consecration, and Communion (1345-1355, 1408).

STEP 4

Forgiveness—
A Story of Love

Celebration of First Reconciliation

★ **Color the boxes using the code to find symbols and a word hidden in the stained glass.**

- • YELLOW
- - RED
- ❖ BROWN
- O PINK
- ▭ ORANGE
- V GREEN

Forgiveness: a gift from God

"Lord, if my brother sins against me, how often must I forgive him?"

From the Bible

THE PARABLE OF THE LOST SON

Luke 15:11-32

Then Jesus said, "A man had two sons, and the younger son said to his father, 'Father, give me the share of your estate that should come to me.' So the father divided the property between them.

After a few days, the younger son collected all his belongings and set off to a distant country where he **wasted all his money** in wild living.

When he had freely spent everything, a severe famine struck that country, and he was left without a thing. So he hired himself out to one of the local farmers who sent him to his farm to take care of his pigs. And he would have been happy to eat what the pigs were eating, but nobody gave him anything. Coming to his senses he thought, 'How many of my father's hired workers have more than enough food to eat, but here am I, dying from hunger.

I shall get up and go to my father and I shall say to him, **'Father, I have sinned against heaven and against you.** I no longer deserve to be called your son; treat me as you would treat one of your hired workers.'

So he got up and went back to his father. While he was still a long way off, his father caught sight of him, and was filled with **compassion**. He ran to his son, embraced him and kissed him.

His son said to him, **'Father, I have sinned against heaven and against you;** I no longer deserve to be called your son.'

But his father ordered his servants, 'Quickly bring the finest robe and put it on him; put a ring on his finger and sandals on his feet.

Take the fattened calf and prepare it. Then let us celebrate with a feast, because **this son of mine was dead, and has come to life again**;

he was lost, and has been found.' Then the celebration began.

Now the older son had been out in the field and, on his way back, as he neared the house, he heard the sound of music and dancing.

He called one of the servants and asked what this might mean.

The servant said to him, 'Your brother has returned, and your father has prepared the fattened calf for a feast because he has him back safe and sound.'

He became angry, and when he refused to enter the house, his father came out and **pleaded** with him.

He said to his father in reply, 'Look, all these years I served you and not once did I disobey your orders; yet you never gave me even a young goat to feast on with my friends.

But when your son returns who wasted your money on bad women, you slaughter the fattened calf for a feast.'

He said to him, 'My son, you are here with me always; everything I have is yours. But now we must celebrate and rejoice, because your brother was dead and has come to life again; **he was lost and has been found.'"**

I don't know how to ask for forgiveness.

When I am forgiven, I am happy!

After a big argument with a friend, it gets better after we begin talking again.

I don't need to ask for forgiveness from my family and friends. They know that I love them!

To forgive is to stop being angry and to find peace in my heart!

Forgiveness is too hard when someone really hurts your feelings.

One time, two times—how many times must I forgive?

Love Justice Happiness Hurt Fight
Sin Justice Fear INJUSTICE Joy Selfishness
JEALOUSY Hope Freedom Lost Pain REUNION Pride
Courage Anger PARTY Worry Patience
Regret REJOICE Forgiveness

There is a bond of love—a constantly renewed covenant—between God and humanity. **Sin** is a choice to do what we know is wrong. Sin hurts this covenant and damages our relationship with God, who loves us unconditionally.

An **accident** is a mistake—the opposite of doing something on purpose.

THINK BACK TO THE PARABLE OF THE LOST SON. UNDERLINE THE WORDS IN YELLOW THAT RELATE TO THE FATHER OF THE TWO SONS, UNDERLINE THE WORDS IN GREEN THAT RELATE TO THE YOUNGER SON, AND UNDERLINE WORDS IN BLUE THAT RELATE TO THE OLDER BROTHER.

Catholic Faith Word

SIN—A free, deliberate choice to turn away from God's love, to break God's law, and to hurt others and ourselves.

Venial versus Mortal Sins

Venial sins are less serious sins, but they still offend God and hurt our relationship with him. Mortal sins, also called deadly sins, are very serious sins. A person who commits a mortal sin knows how wrong the sin is. Mortal sins completely separate us from God and must be confessed to receive forgiveness.

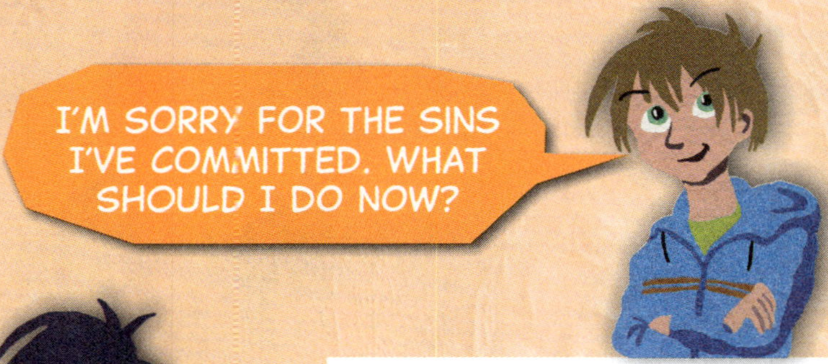

The Sacrament of Reconciliation

The Sacrament of **Reconciliation** repairs our broken relationship with our Lord and with the Church. In this sacrament, we show sorrow for our sins and promise to turn away from sin in the future. The priest forgives our sins in the name of Jesus. The Lord has provided this sacrament as a way for us to return to God and the Church. We celebrate God's forgiveness of our unloving choices.

Catholic Faith Word

RECONCILIATION—The sacrament in which we confess our sins, receive God's forgiveness, and do penance for our sins.

Examination Of Conscience

Before the Sacrament of Reconciliation, we take time to think about the times we have failed to love God and others. This reflection time is called an **examination of conscience**, which helps us prepare ourselves to tell the priest our sins and ask God for mercy and forgiveness.

Catholic Faith Word

EXAMINATION OF CONSCIENCE– Preparing for the Sacrament of Reconciliation by thinking about the sins we have committed.

Do I keep God's commandments?

1. Do I try to love God with my whole heart?
2. Do I use God's name for praying and not swear God's name for fun or in anger?
3. Do I worship God at Mass on Sunday?
4. Do I show respect for my parents and other adults who take care of me?
5. Have I been mean to anyone?
6. Have I done anything to hurt my own or someone else's body?
7. Have I taken or destroyed things that belong to others?
8. Do I tell the truth?
9. Have I been jealous of what others have?
10. Have I been jealous of another person's family or lifestyle?

Do I act like Jesus?

1. Do I share with others?
2. Do I help when people ask me?
3. Do I forgive instead of trying to get even?
4. Do I ask lonely children to play?
5. Do I keep promises?
6. Do I treat other children fairly?
7. Do I obey my parents?
8. Do I treat other children with respect?

Look at the illustrations. Reflect on the times you have hurt God or others.

PREPARING FOR YOUR FIRST RECONCILIATION...

You're getting ready to meet Jesus Christ!

Who are you talking to?

The priest puts on his white alb and purple stole. Sitting face-to-face or behind a screen, he greets you in the name of Jesus. Acting as Christ, the priest listens as you confess your sins.

What do you say to the priest?

Tell the priest your sins: the actions that have hurt others or that have turned you away from the love of God.

The Sacrament of Reconciliation: Step-by-Step

Welcoming in the name of Jesus

- Greet the priest and make the **Sign of the Cross** together.
- The priest invites you to trust in God. He might read a short passage from the Bible.
- **Tell** the priest that it's your first confession (or how long it's been since your last confession). For example, say, "Bless me, Father, for I have sinned. It has been [say how long] since my last confession. These are my sins."

Confession of sins

- Tell the priest your **sins**.
- Show sorrow (or repentance) for your sins by saying a prayer called the **Act of Contrition**. (Examples are in the yellow box.)
- Listen to the **penance** that the priest gives you. Then, the priest offers you God's forgiveness through the Prayer of **Absolution**:
  God, the Father of mercies,
  through the Death and Resurrection of his Son
  has reconciled the world to himself
  and poured out the Holy Spirit for the forgiveness of sins;
  through the ministry of the Church
  may God grant you pardon and peace.
  And I absolve you from your sins,
  In the name of the Father, and of the Son, and of the Holy Spirit.
  (*Order of Penance*)
- Make the **Sign of the Cross** and say **"Amen."**
- Thank the priest as you leave. Make sure to **do your penance** as soon as you can.

Catholic Faith Word

PENANCE–An act that shows sorrow and repentance for sin.

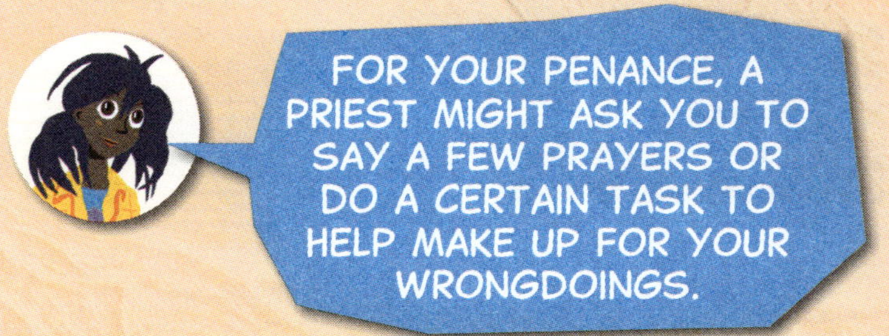

ACT OF CONTRITION
(THESE OR SIMILAR WORDS)

O my God,
I am sorry and repent with all my heart
for all the wrong I have done
and for the good I have failed to do,
because by sinning I have offended you,
who are all good and worthy to be loved above all things.
I firmly resolve, with the help of your grace,
to do penance,
to sin no more,
and to avoid the occasions of sin.
Through the merits of the Passion of our Savior Jesus Christ,
Lord, have mercy.
Amen.

OR

Lord Jesus, Son of God,
have mercy on me, a sinner.
Amen.
(Order of Penance)

(See pages 70-73 for more Act of Contrition options and step-by-step instructions with photos.)

Your sins are forgiven!

My heart is filled with **joy** because you understand me. I know you won't abandon me when I call for help. you are patient with me.

You love me like a **Father.** You give me strength and joy. Thank you, Lord. Amen.

Lord, your love for us is so big that we will never be able to measure it! You accept us as we are; when we do something wrong and we ask your forgiveness, you do not scold us. You **open your arms,** and look at us with tenderness.

You put us back on our feet, and you encourage us to go forward with a brand new heart. Blessed are you, Lord, for **showering your love upon us.** Amen.

My God, your way is sure. I know you're there!

I know that I can count on you.

I know that you love me.

In the depths of my heart, you teach me what is wise and true. **Thank you,** Lord. Amen.

With you, Lord, I truly exist. You love me and know me inside out.

I want to **praise** you, I want to sing to you, because you never fail to show me your love.

I told you my sins and you forgave me. Your **love** is forever. I'm counting on you. Give me the strength to live through all my days. Amen.

Thank you Lord, for this friendship, for the **peace** that you give us.

Help us to share this friendship and this **peace with those** around us. Amen.

Choose a prayer to thank God for his forgiveness.

WITH MY FAMILY

Discuss

Talk about forgiveness in your family: What signs or words can you choose together to express forgiveness? What resolutions can you make to avoid hurting others and to live in love?

____

____

____

____

____

CATECHISM Q&A

Q Which sins must be confessed?

A A person must confess to a priest all grave (mortal) sins he or she remembers after having carefully examined his or her conscience. The confession of serious sins is the only ordinary way to obtain forgiveness. Confessing venial faults is strongly recommended by the Church (1456).

Do-It-Yourself Craft

The father welcomed his son into his merciful arms **(Luke 15:11-32)**. This interactive card will remind you of God's forgiveness!

1. Cut a cardboard strip 6 inches x 1 ½ inches, and mark the folds 1 ½ inches from the edge.

2. Cut a right hand and a left hand out of yellow cardboard, and glue them at each end. Cut a 1 ½ inch circle, and draw your face.

3. Cut a 3 inch x 1 inch strip and write the text: *Like the father of the lost son, God embraces me and forgives me.*

4. Finish assembling the card.

First Communion Bus
STEP 5
Invited to the Banquet

Find the missing words using the definitions. (These words have been mentioned in the first four steps.)

Definitions:

1. a plant on which grapes grow
2. a man ordained in the Sacrament of Holy Orders who has the power to forgive sins in the name of Jesus
3. the Son of God
4. the sacrament that makes us children of God and members of God's family, the Church
5. an invitation from Christ to live as a child of God
6. a feeling of deep tenderness and care
7. the Church's central act of public worship
8. an agreement of faith and love between God and his people
9. forgiveness or compassion

The words in the green boxes relate to a Bible story about a feast—but the vowels are missing. Find these 7 words, and write them on the lines below.

To help you, here's a code:

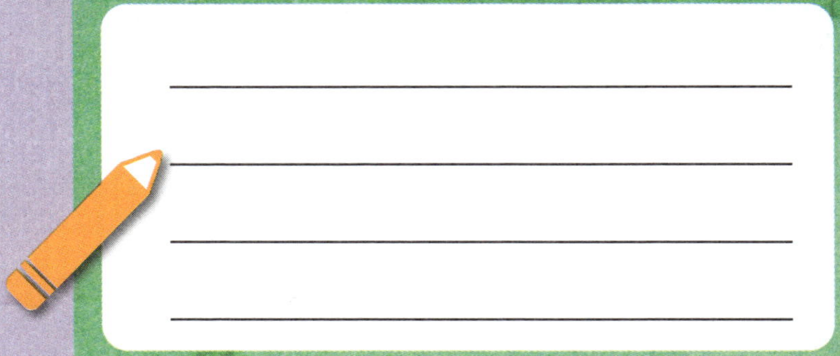

From the Bible

THE WEDDING AT CANA

John 2:1-11

On the third day there was a wedding in Cana in Galilee, and the mother of Jesus was there.

Jesus and his disciples were also invited to the wedding.

When the wine ran out, the mother of Jesus said to him, "They have no wine." Jesus said to her, "How does this affect me? My time has not yet come."

His mother said to the servers, **"Do whatever he tells you."**

Now there were six stone water jars there for Jewish ceremonial washings, each able to hold twenty to thirty gallons of water.

Jesus told them, **"Fill the jars with water."** So they filled them to the brim.

Then he told them, "Draw some out now and take it to the headwaiter."* So they took it.

And when the headwaiter tasted **the water that had become wine,** without knowing where it came from (although the servers who had drawn the water knew), the headwaiter called the bridegroom and said to him, "Everyone serves good wine first, and then when people have had plenty to drink, a less tasty wine is served; but you have saved the best wine until now."

Jesus did this as the beginning of his **signs** in Cana in Galilee and so revealed his glory, and his disciples began to believe in him.

A Sign?

Saint John does not say how Jesus transforms water into wine. Jesus simply acts, and by his words, the water becomes wine.

A **SIGN**, or miracle, attracts attention; it shows something important.

The miracle at Cana reveals that Jesus is the long-awaited Messiah!

The Tale of the Water Carrier and the Cracked Jar

God fills us with many gifts. Which gifts can I share to make the world more beautiful and to bring joy to others? Write one or more of these gifts inside your jar and decorate it.

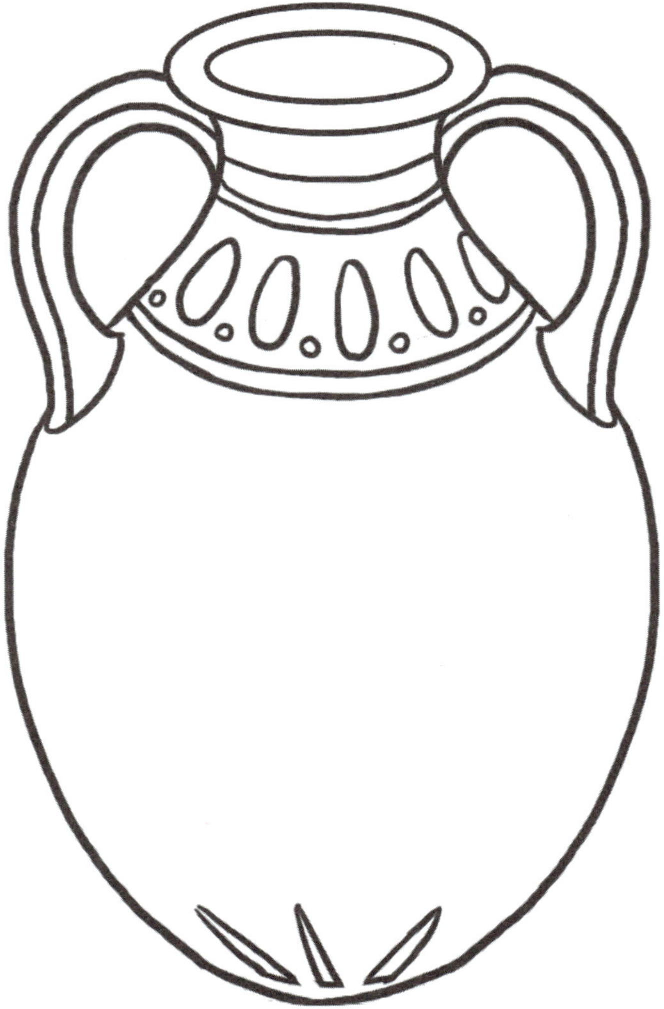

AT CHURCH

COME TO THE TABLE OF THE LORD!

The Order of Mass

Liturgy of the Eucharist

- **PREPARATION OF THE ALTAR, COLLECTION, AND PROCESSION WITH GIFTS:** Members of the assembly bring the gifts of bread and wine to the altar. The collection of money supports the Church and is shared with people in need.
- **PRAYER OVER THE OFFERINGS:** The priest prays that the gifts may be acceptable to God.

Jesus invites us to be nourished by His Body and Blood!

THE LORD'S SUPPER

From the Bible

Matthew 26:26-29

While they were eating, Jesus **took bread** said the blessing, **broke it**, and giving it to his disciples said, "**Take and eat; this is my body**." Then he **took a cup**, gave thanks, and gave it to them, saying, "**Drink from it**, all of you, for **this is my blood of the covenant**, which will be shed on behalf of many for the forgiveness of sins. I tell you, from now on I shall not drink this fruit of the vine until the day when I drink it with you new in the kingdom of my Father."

Catholic Faith Word

LITURGY OF THE EUCHARIST—The second part of the Mass, during which the bread and wine truly become the Body and Blood of Christ.

LITURGY OF THE EUCHARIST (CONTINUED)

The Eucharistic Prayer

- **PREFACE:** The priest says a prayer of thanksgiving for all the wonderful deeds God has done throughout history and in our own lives.
- **SANCTUS:** We sing praises about the greatness and the infinite love of God by singing, "Holy, Holy, Holy, Lord God of hosts!"
- **CONSECRATION:** The priest extends his hands and asks the Father to send the Holy Spirit on the gifts of bread and wine so that they may become the Body and Blood of Christ. This complete change of the bread and wine into the Body and Blood of Jesus is called **transubstantiation**.
- **MEMORIAL ACCLAMATION:** We proclaim the mystery of our faith: through his Death and Resurrection, Christ has set us free.
- **AMEN:** By saying "Amen," we express belief that Jesus is with us, present in the Eucharist.

The Communion Rite

- **LORD'S PRAYER:** We join our voices together saying the prayer that Jesus taught us—the Our Father.
- **RITE OF PEACE:** The priest invites us to share a sign of Christ's peace (usually a handshake) with others nearby.
- **THE BREAKING OF THE BREAD AND THE LAMB OF GOD:** The priest breaks the large Host, and he repeats the actions of Jesus. By singing the Lamb of God, we ask Jesus, the Lamb sacrificed to save us from sin, to have mercy on us, and give us peace.
- **COMMUNION:** We come forward to receive the Body and Blood of Christ.

Concluding Rites

- **BLESSING:** The priest or bishop blesses us in the name of the Father, Son, and Holy Spirit.
- **DISMISSAL:** Reminded of our mission to love and serve the Lord, we sing joyfully as we are sent forth to proclaim the Good News.

Catholic Faith Word

TRANSUBSTANTIATION–The changing of the bread and wine into the Body and Blood of Jesus Christ in the Sacrament of the Eucharist.

Let's walk through the Mass together!

INTRODUCTORY RITES

Enter the celebration

1 Entrance Procession

3 Penitential Act

4 Gloria

2 Sign of the Cross and Greeting

5 Collect

LITURGY OF THE WORD

6 Readings and Psalm

8 Homily

10 Prayer of the Faithful

7 Gospel Acclamation and Gospel Reading

9 Profession of Faith

Listen to God's Word

LITURGY OF THE EUCHARIST

11 Preparation of the Altar, Collection, and Procession with Gifts

12 Prayer over the Offerings

13 Eucharistic Prayer

14 Lord's Prayer

15 Lamb of God

16 Communion

Remember and give thanks for Christ's sacrifice

CONCLUDING RITES

Go forth and live out the Gospel

17 Blessing

18 Dismissal

As we get closer to our destination—the day of your First Communion—why do you personally want to receive Jesus in the Eucharist? Has anything changed for you since your journey started?

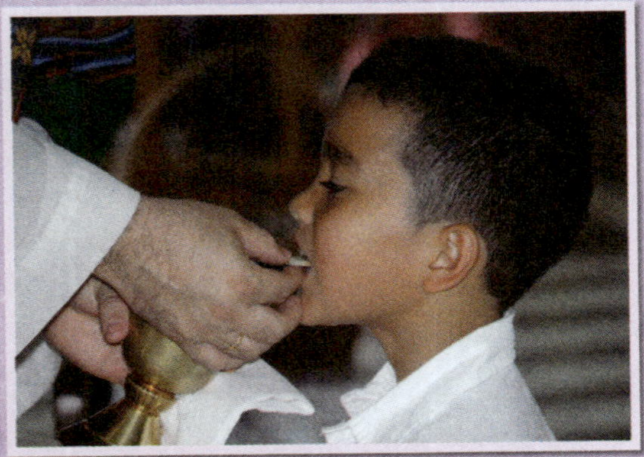

Pray with Saint Charles de Foucauld

My father,

I surrender to You,

do what you want with me.

Whatever you do with me, I'll thank you.

I am ready for anything, I accept everything.

May your will be done in me,

As in all creatures,

I desire nothing more, my God.

I give my soul into your hands.

I give it to you, my God,

with all the love of my heart,

because I love you,

and that I need to give myself,

to put myself in your hands,

without measure,

with infinite confidence,

for you are my Father.

Amen.

WITH MY FAMILY — Discuss

Ask your parents or godparents what they remember about the day they celebrated their First Eucharist. Write their memories on the lines below.

....

....

....

....

....

....

....

....

....

CATECHISM Q&A

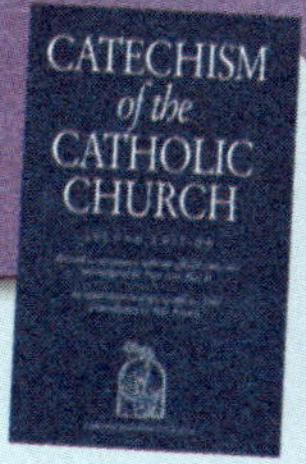

Q In what way is the Eucharist a memorial of the sacrifice of Christ?

A The Eucharist is a memorial because it makes present Jesus' sacrifice on the Cross—which was offered once and for all on behalf of all humanity. We hear this in the very words of institution, "This is my Body which is given for you" and "This cup is the New Covenant in my Blood that will be shed for you" (Luke 22:19-20). The sacrifice of the Cross and the sacrifice of the Eucharist are the same sacrifice (1362-1367).

STEP 6

At the Lord's Table

Celebration of First Eucharist

Sacred vessels used at Mass

CHALICE
This cup holds the wine that is consecrated during Mass and becomes the Blood of Christ.

A CRUCIFIX is placed on the altar or next to it. It reminds us of Jesus' Death and Resurrection.

PATEN
The priest's host and those of the assembly are put on this plate and presented on the altar.

The altar is covered with a white altar cloth. Sometimes, the altar cloth shows an image of a lamb, representing Jesus, the Lamb of God, who came to save us from sin and death.

CRUETS
Small bottles containing the water and the wine are poured into the chalice.

CIBORIUM
This sacred vessel contains the consecrated Hosts (which have become the Body of Christ) that are distributed during Communion. Closed with a lid, the ciborium holds the leftover consecrated Hosts in the tabernacle.

Catholic Faith Word

TABERNACLE–A small, locked box where consecrated Hosts are kept. Nearby, a red sanctuary lamp is lit to show that Jesus is present.

Liturgy of the Eucharist: Mass Responses to Know

AT CHURCH

Invitation to Prayer

THE PRIEST SAYS: Pray, brothers and sisters, that my sacrifice and yours may be acceptable to God, the almighty Father.

WE RESPOND: May the Lord accept the sacrifice at your hands for the praise and glory of his name, for our good and the good of all his holy Church.

Preface Dialogue

THE PRIEST SAYS:
The Lord be with you.

WE RESPOND:
And with your spirit.

THE PRIEST SAYS:
Lift up your hearts.

WE RESPOND:
We lift them up to the Lord.

THE PRIEST SAYS:
Let us give thanks to the Lord our God.

WE RESPOND:
It is right and just.

Liturgy of the Eucharist: More Mass Responses to Know

Responses We Sing During the Liturgy of the Eucharist:

SANCTUS:

Holy, Holy, Holy Lord God of hosts.
Heaven and earth are full of your glory.
Hosanna in the highest.
Blessed is he who comes in the name of the Lord.
Hosanna in the highest.

MEMORIAL ACCLAMATION:

We proclaim your Death, O Lord, and profess your Resurrection until you come again.
or When we eat this Bread and drink this Cup, we proclaim your death, O Lord, until you come again.
or Save us, Savior of the world, for by your Cross and Resurrection you have set us free.

THE GREAT AMEN:

Amen.

LAMB OF GOD:

Lamb of God, you take away the sins of the world, have mercy on us. (Repeat.)
Lamb of God, you take away the sins of the world, grant us peace.

Invitation to Communion

THE PRIEST SAYS:

Behold the Lamb of God,
behold him who takes away the sins of the world.
Blessed are those called to the supper of the Lamb.

WE RESPOND:

Lord, I am not worthy
that you should enter under my roof,
but only say the word
and my soul shall be healed.

RECEIVING HOLY COMMUNION

- **Walk forward** in the Communion procession toward the priest or Eucharistic minister.
- When you are about to receive Communion, **bow your head** as a sign of reverence.
- To receive the Body of Christ in your hands, hands: put your left hand in the palm of your right hand, palms up (or right hand in the palm of your left hand, if you are left-handed). The priest, deacon, or extraordinary minister of Holy Communion will say, **"The Body of Christ."** You respond, **"Amen."** The Body of Christ will be placed in your hand. Pick up the Host with your other hand and put it on your tongue. Close your mouth and swallow.
- To receive the Body of Christ on your tongue: The priest, deacon, or extraordinary minister of Holy Communion will say, **"The Body of Christ."** You respond, **"Amen."** Then open your mouth and put your tongue out. The priest or minister will put the Body of Christ on your tongue. Close your mouth and swallow.
- To receive the Blood of Christ, the priest, deacon, or extraordinary minister of Holy Communion will say, **"The Blood of Christ."** You respond, **"Amen."** The priest or minister will give you the chalice. Take it and drink a sip from it. Then hand the chalice back.
- Return to your place and **kneel** down.
- Say a **thank-you prayer** in your own words for Jesus coming to you in Holy Communion. Sing the Communion song.

"In approaching therefore, come not with your wrists extended, or your fingers spread; but make your left hand a throne for the right, as for that which is to receive a King. And having hollowed your palm, receive the Body of Christ, saying over it, Amen."

The Fifth Mystagogical Catechesis of Saint Cyril of Jerusalem

Is the Eucharist really Jesus' Body and Blood?

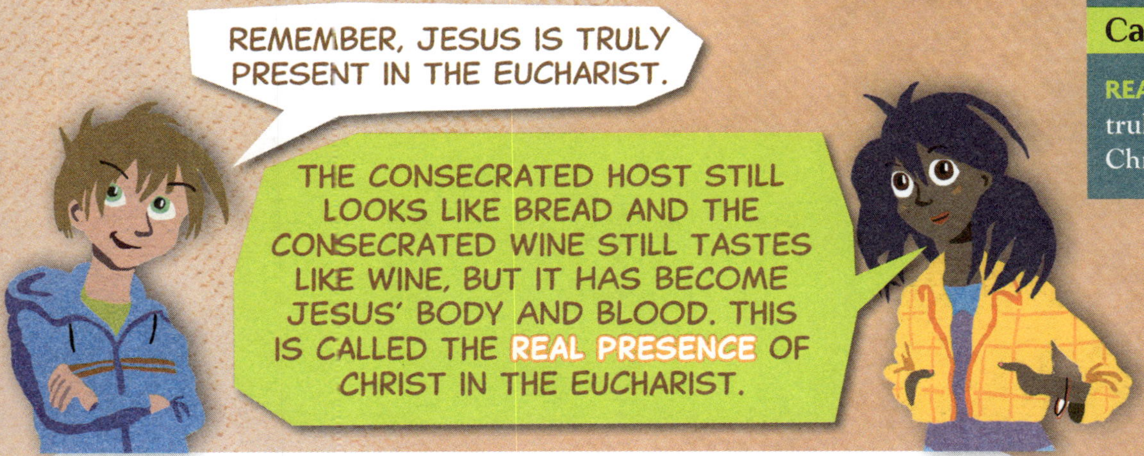

Each time we receive the Eucharist, we become one with Christ. We proclaim that we are saved by the sacrifice of Jesus' Death on the Cross and his glorious Resurrection.

CATECHISM Q&A

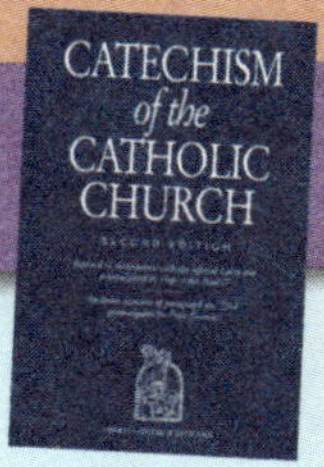

Q How is Christ present in the Eucharist?

A Jesus Christ is present in the Eucharist in a true, real, and substantial way: with his Body and his Blood, with his Soul and his Divinity. Under the appearance of bread and wine, Christ is truly present—wholly and entirely, God and man (1373-1375, 1413).

Catholic Faith Word

REAL PRESENCE–The bread and wine truly become the Body and Blood of Christ at Mass.

WITH MY FAMILY Pray

As your First Holy Communion day approaches, pray this prayer as a family.

Jesus, at every Mass, you are there. You are truly present in the Eucharist. Nourish me so that you can work through me and help me to be more like you. Amen.

STEP 7

Entering into the Mysteries

We have arrived!

Write down some favorite discoveries or memories from your First Communion journey.

The adventure continues...

The Sacraments of Christian Initiation:

Three sacraments that welcome us into the full life of the Church

1 **Baptism (received once)**

THE PRIEST SAYS:

"I baptize you in the name of the Father, and of the Son, and of the Holy Spirit."

Confirmation (received once) **2**

THE BISHOP SAYS:

"Be sealed by the Holy Spirit, the gift of God."

3 **Eucharist (received at least every Sunday)**

THE PRIEST SAYS:

"The Body of Christ."

Catholic Faith Word

SACRAMENTS–Visible signs of invisible grace instituted by Christ and given to the Church.

The Church has seven ***sacraments****. Each of the sacraments gives us a share in God's life. Sharing in God's life is called grace.*

EUCHARIST		
CONFIRMATION	RECONCILIATION	MARRIAGE
BAPTISM	ANOINTING OF THE SICK	HOLY ORDERS
Entering into Christian life	*Healing for the body and soul*	*Building up the human family and the mission of the Church*

Be Christ's Witnesses to the World!

EACH SUNDAY, THE CHURCH INVITES ME TO GROW AS A CHRISTIAN BY:

- RENEWING THE COVENANT OF MY BAPTISM WITH THE FATHER, SON, AND HOLY SPIRIT
- LISTENING TO GOD'S WORD SO THAT I CAN REMAIN CONNECTED TO JESUS
- NOURISHING MYSELF WITH THE BODY AND BLOOD OF CHRIST TO BE STRENGTHENED ON MY JOURNEY OF FAITH.

LIVING A CHRISTIAN LIFE MAKES YOU A POWERFUL **WITNESS** TO THE GOSPEL. SPREAD THE GOOD NEWS NOT ONLY THROUGH YOUR WORDS, BUT ALSO THROUGH YOUR ACTIONS!

TELL OTHERS ABOUT YOUR JOURNEY—THIS COULD MAKE THEM WANT TO START THEIR ADVENTURE.

The Profession of Faith

At Sunday Mass, we, the Church family, profess our faith by saying the Creed. We say that we believe in God, in his Son, Jesus Christ, in the Holy Spirit, and in the Church. When we do this, we renew our baptismal promises—uniting us with our entire Church family!

Catholic Faith Word

WITNESS– A person who shows through words and actions that he or she is follower of Christ.

Example of *Prayer After Communion*

May this divine sacrifice we have offered and received fill us with life, O Lord, we pray, so that, bound to you in lasting charity, we may bear fruit that lasts forever. Through Christ our Lord. Amen.

Discuss

Think of the words you have heard in the Prayer after Communion, near the end of Mass. Write your family's definition of Communion.

....

....

....

....

PRAYER

Lord, as I continue on this journey toward full participation in the life of the Church, unite myself to you and help me be a witness of your mighty love. Give me the courage to spread the Good News everywhere I go. Amen.

CATECHISM Q&A

Q What are the sacraments of Christian Initiation and what do they do?

A The sacraments of Christian initiation lay the foundations of Christian life. The faithful born anew by Baptism are strengthened by Confirmation and are then nourished by the Eucharist (1212, 1275).

Fill in the missing letters to discover some of the Catholic Faith Words you have learned throughout this journey.

R___conciliation

___iturgy of the Eucha___ist

Bap___ism

___enance

c___venant

Gos___els

Litur___y of the Wor___

C___urch

sacram___nts

ta___ernacle

e___amination of ___onscience

wit___ess

Rea___ P___esence

Baptism
The sacrament that makes us children of God and members of God's family, the Church

Church
The People of God gathered in the name of Jesus Christ.

covenant
A commitment or agreement of faith and love between God and his people.

Eucharist
The sacrament in which we receive Jesus' Body and Blood to nourish us and help us to become more like him.

examination of conscience
Preparing for the Sacrament of Reconciliation by thinking about the sins we have committed.

Gospels
The first four books in the New Testament that tell the Good News of Jesus' life, Death, and Resurrrection.

Liturgy of the Word
One of the two main parts of the Mass, during which we hear God's Word from the Bible and reflect on what it means for our lives.

Liturgy of the Eucharist
The second part of the Mass, during which the bread and wine truly become the Body and Blood of Christ.

Mass
The Catholic Church's central act of public worship.

penance
An act that shows sorrow and repentance for sin.

Real Presence
The bread and wine truly become the Body and Blood of Christ at Mass.

Reconciliation
The sacrament in which we confess our sins, receive God's forgiveness, and do penance for our sins.

sacraments
Visible signs of invisible grace instituted by Christ and given to the Church.

sin
A free, deliberate choice to turn away from God's love, to break God's law, and to hurt others and ourselves.

tabernacle
A small, locked box where the consecrated Hosts are kept. Nearby, a red sanctuary lamp is lit to show that Jesus is present.

transubstantiation
The changing of the bread and wine into the Body and Blood of Jesus Christ in the Sacrament of the Eucharist.

witness
A person who shows through words and actions that he or she is a follower of Christ.

Word of God
Another word for the Bible or Scripture.

FAQ Questions Parents Ask about First Reconciliation

Q What Are the Sacraments of Healing?

A The Sacrament of Penance and Reconciliation (or Confession) and the Sacrament of Anointing of the Sick continue Jesus' work of healing and saving the world through the power of the Holy Spirit.

Q What can my child understand about sin and reconciliation at this young age?

A The Church prepares and welcomes children to First Penance and First Communion when they reach the age of reason. They are at the right age to begin learning the commandments that make us God's people.

The Ten Commandments put us in relationship with God, who leads and loves us and who deserves our worship and thanks. The commandments call us to become people who respect one another's lives, reputations, marriages, and property. When we break one of the commandments or commit sin, we must heal our relationship with God through the Sacrament of Reconciliation. This program stresses God's forgiving love by examining the Parable of the Lost Son, where children learn that God our Father will welcome us back into his loving embrace when we show repentance for our sins.

Q What is my part in preparing my child for First Reconciliation?

A Both the family and the parish have important roles in preparing children for First Reconciliation. Parishes expect parents to do all they can to connect their child's understanding of following Jesus' teachings with keeping family rules.

For example, children need to understand that doing their chores is a way of keeping the Fourth Commandment to honor parents. Not going to bed angry is a family rule that flows from Jesus' teaching in his Sermon on the Mount about not going to the Temple to worship without first making up with an angry friend.

Parents can also help their children by modeling a willingness to say "I'm sorry." They can acknowledge when they are wrong or misread a situation among their children. They can help their children develop practical peacemaking skills at home. Parents can also help their children learn the Act of Contrition and the Lord's Prayer

Q What help does *Invited by Christ* give me in my role as a parent of a child preparing for First Reconciliation?

A *Invited by Christ* provides several sources of support and involvement for parents. This special parent appendix answers questions parents frequently ask and seeks to update them on the theology of Reconciliation.

Second, this book includes a "With My Family" section at the end of each stepage Parents and their children can do these activities together as part of the child's preparation.

Q Is my child required to celebrate First Reconciliation before celebrating First Eucharist?

A The Church requires children to receive the Sacrament of Reconciliation before receiving First Eucharist. Parishes prepare and celebrate this sacrament with children a significant length of time before they prepare children for First Eucharist, so children do not receive the impression they must go to Confession before they go to Communion each time.

Church law commands us to lead a sacramental life, to receive the Sacrament of Reconciliation regularly. Church law requires Catholics to receive the Sacrament of Reconciliation at least once a year minimally, although confession is obligatory only if serious sin is involved.

Q Why should I prepare my child for Reconciliation?

A Because your child is coming to the age when parishes prepare children for First Reconciliation, it offers you, as parents, a chance to update your own understanding of the sacrament. We recognize that every Eucharist includes penitential prayers. We begin with a Penitential Rite in which we ask forgiveness and mercy for our sins. Every Gospel challenges us to deeper conversion. We also pray the Lord's Prayer at every Eucharist, asking to be forgiven our trespasses as we forgive others. We offer one another signs of peace before we receive Communion. However, only in sacramental confession is one ordinarily absolved from mortal or serious sins.

In the very early centuries of the Church, people regarded the Sacrament of Reconciliation as a second Baptism and received it only once in their lifetime. To receive the sacrament, people became public penitents for a period of time. Usually they did this only in the case of grave sin such as murder or adultery. Just as the waters of Baptism cleansed Christians of original sin, so the tears of repentance washed away all personal sin. The practice of frequent confession grew in the Middle Ages to give people more help in transforming their lives.

Without being strictly necessary, confession of everyday faults (venial sins) helps us to form our consciences, fight against temptations, be healed by Christ, and make progress in living as a follower of Christ (*CCC*, 1458).

Q What will my child learn about right and wrong from *Invited By Christ*?

A *Invited By Christ* works at helping children distinguish loving from unloving actions.

An examination of conscience for children is provided in Step 4. Children ask themselves, "Do I keep God's commandments?" The questions are put concretely and positively in children's terms.

1. Do I try to love God with my whole heart?
2. Do I use God's name for praying and not swear God's name for fun or in anger?
3. Do I worship God at Mass on Sunday?
4. Do I show respect for my parents and other adults who take care of me?
5. Have I been mean to anyone?
6. Have I done anything to hurt my own or someone else's body?
7. Have I taken or destroyed things that belong to others?
8. Do I tell the truth?
9. Have I been jealous of what others have?
10. Have I been jealous of another person's family or lifestyle?

Children also ask themselves the question, "Do I act like Jesus?" These questions, too, concretely and positively express in children's terms what Jesus asks.

1. Do I share with others?
2. Do I help when people ask me?
3. Do I forgive instead of trying to get even?
4. Do I ask lonely children to play?
5. Do I keep promises?
6. Do I treat other children fairly?
7. Do I obey my parents?
8. Do I treat other children with respect?

Questions Parents Ask about First Reconciliation

Children who complete the *Invited by Christ* First Penance program will not be finished learning right from wrong. Instruction as children grow up includes a continuing call to conversion and learning of right and wrong appropriate to their age level.

Q Why do we call Confession *Reconciliation*?

A Confessing our sins is only one of the four main actions in the Sacrament of Reconciliation. The other three include sorrow for our sins, doing penance to make up for our wrongs and to make peace with those we have hurt, and absolution.

The *Catechism of the Catholic Church* tells us that the Sacrament of Reconciliation is another name for the Sacrament of Penance because the sacrament "imparts to the sinner the love of God who reconciles: "Be reconciled to God." He who lives by God's merciful love is ready to respond to the Lord's call: "Go; first be reconciled to your brother" (*CCC*, 1424).

The practice of calling this sacrament the Sacrament of Reconciliation expresses the whole purpose of the Sacrament. It aims not only to forgive and take away sin but to heal our relations with God and with one another.

Q How is the Sacrament of Reconciliation celebrated and what happens in this sacrament?

A Vatican II directed many changes in the rites of the sacraments. The Sacrament of Reconciliation is usually celebrated in one of two forms. In addition to private confession, there are also communal services with common prayer before individual confession.

Those receiving this sacrament must take four steps. First, they must be sincerely sorry for their sins and have the firm purpose of sinning no more. Second, they must confess their sins to a priest. Third, they must be willing to make amends for harm caused by the sins committed. Fourth, they must receive absolution, or forgiveness, from the priest. In the Sacrament of Reconciliation, the priest forgives sins in the name and person of Christ himself, just as the priest who consecrates the bread and wine at Mass does so through the power of Christ.

A person prepares mentally and spiritually for this sacrament just as an athlete prepares physically for a game. To get ready for confession, a person examines his or her conscience. That means to recall all the sins committed since his or her last confession. In doing so, the person must take special notice of any mortal sins because these must be confessed to the priest.

After a priest hears someone's confession, he always assigns an action the person must take to make up for his or her sins. It might be saying some prayers or doing a good deed. This act is called a penance, and the Sacrament of Penance and Reconciliation is not complete until the person has completed the penance.

The sacrament has six positive effects. First, it restores the sinner's broken relationship with God. Second, it also restores the sinner's broken relationship with God's family, the Church. Third, it ensures the sinner's salvation from eternal punishment. Fourth, it gives the sinner peace of mind. Fifth, it goes even further and gives the sinner joy in Christ. Finally, it increases the sinner's spiritual strength, which is important for avoiding future sin.

Q Why is there an option for a communal celebration of the Sacrament of Penance?

A Communal celebrations of the sacrament express the reality that all Christians sin and need to open their hearts to conversion. At these services, the Church calls us to stand together and hear the Word of God, in which is reechoed our basic Christian call to be holy as God is holy, to be forgiving as God forgives us, to be peacemakers as Jesus called us to be. The Holy Spirit, Jesus' gift to his followers on Easter evening, works in each of us and in all of us together to teach us ways of making peace.

At a communal celebration, a priest can develop a homily on the Scriptures that calls many people at once to conversion. We can recite a litany of sins together that acknowledges that many of our failures to love are the same and are part of our daily interaction with one another. In a communal setting, Catholics also confess serious, personal sins to a priest in private.

Parishes usually hold communal reconciliation services during Advent and Lent and enhance the celebrations with music and symbols of repentance. Communal celebrations tend to have great power to affect our hearts and renew our commitment to transformation in Christ.

Q What Is Sin?

A Sin is disobedience. It is any word, deed, or desire that breaks God's Law. A serious act of disobedience is called a mortal sin. Three things make a sin mortal. First, the sin concerns a serious matter. Second, the person recognizes how serious the sin is. Third, the person freely chooses to commit the sin anyway. An example is taking weeks to plan a murder, then carrying it out. Committing a mortal sin in effect is choosing eternal death. If the sinner does not repent, he or she cannot enter into eternal life with God in Heaven.

Venial sin is a lesser offense against God's Law. While it is also wrong, it does not bring eternal punishment. Examples of venial sin include such things as hitting someone in anger, lying about something small, or stealing a small sum of money.

However, venial sins can still be dangerous. Repeating the same venial sin over and over can put a person at risk of falling into mortal sin. For example, it is a venial sin for someone to want revenge when he or she has been hurt by another person. But thinking every day about ways of getting even can lead to planning an actual attack and even carrying out that attack. Harming another person, that person's reputation, loved ones, or property to get revenge would be committing a mortal sin.

Q Can my child understand what a mortal sin is?

A A mortal sin is any serious sin committed while knowing how wrong the sin is. An obvious example of a mortal sin is intentionally killing someone, although other mortal sins include lying about another in court or stealing all the money another has to live on.

Once children reach the age of reason, they are capable of grave sin. Children clearly need to know the grave sins the Ten Commandments forbid. However, young children are not always capable of the full knowledge, consent, and intent that constitutes a grave mortal sin.

Children will need help distinguishing between accidents and actions they intend as well as between serious or mortal sin and venial sin. Children's concrete thinking ability limits their capacity to foresee consequences and put themselves in others' shoes.

FAQ Questions Parents Ask about First Reconciliation

Baptism calls all Christians to lifelong conversion, of which preparing for First Reconciliation is an initial stepage The *Catechism* teaches that "after having attained the age of discretion, each of the faithful is bound by an obligation faithfully to confess serious sins at least once a year" (*CCC*, 1457). The Church recommends, but does not demand, that venial sins also be confessed.

Q What impact will *Together in Jesus* have on my child?

A The program aims to help children appreciate that God, who gifts them with life, loves them and lavishly forgives their mistakes and sins. The program presents Reconciliation as a sacrament that calls our priests to continue Jesus' healing and forgiving ministry among us and our Church to be a peacemaking, reconciling community.

Q What if my child doesn't want to participate in First Reconciliation?

A In preparing children for this Sacrament of Healing, parents and catechists must pay attention to a child's own desires and feelings. Parents should talk over the plans with their children and alert the catechist if their child needs some special assurance or information.

Encourage your child to take part in preparation with the other children, so they know how to receive the sacrament. First Reconciliation programs make reconciliation services celebrations of God's love for the children. In all likelihood, your child's experience will be positive.

However, if your child still doesn't wish to receive First Reconciliation, accept his or her wishes for now. Talk with your pastor or parish director of faith formation about options for your child. Perhaps he or she can join in the program at a later date.

Questions Parents Ask about First Eucharist

Q What Are the Sacraments of Christian Initiation?

A Sacraments are signs instituted by Christ to give grace, which is a share in the life of God. The Church celebrates the sacraments through visible rites that make real what they signify. For example, the rite for Baptism includes the use of water and the reciting of the baptismal formula. This rite both cleanses a person of sin and claims the person for God. It brings about what it signifies.

Do you know what it means to be initiated into a club? It is to be welcomed into the club through taking part in a ceremony, such as raising the right hand and reciting a pledge. Three of the Church's sacraments are called Sacraments of Initiation because they welcome a person into the full life of the Church. These sacraments are Baptism, Confirmation, and Eucharist. Through Baptism, a person begins a new life in Christ. Confirmation strengthens that new life. Through Eucharist, the person is nourished by Christ's Body and Blood in order to be transformed in Christ.

In the first centuries, when most new members of the Church were adults, all three sacraments were administered at the same time—first Baptism, then Confirmation, then Eucharist. In later centuries, however, when new members often were babies and as the Church grew, the three Sacraments of Initiation were celebrated at different times so bishops *could continue to complete Baptism in the celebration of Confirmation.*

Q What Happens at the Eucharist?

A Unlike Baptism and Confirmation, the Eucharist is a sacrament that can be received again and again. In fact, the Church encourages Catholics to receive Eucharist every time they attend Mass. At the very least, they are required to receive Eucharist at least once a year, during the Easter season. Receiving Communion once a year is a Church rule. Attending Mass is a serious obligation that flows from the Third Commandment; a deliberate choice to miss Sunday Mass is considered a mortal sin. When you seek strength from Christ's Body and Blood during Sunday Mass, you become better at resisting serious sin during the rest of the week.

There is no other sacrament quite like the Eucharist. The *Catechism* calls it "the heart and the summit of the Church's life." The Eucharist is the heart because it is at the center of the Church's life. It is the summit because it is higher than any other form of worship or prayer.

Receiving the Body and Blood of Christ in Holy Communion is necessary for a healthy spiritual life. You need Eucharist as much as you need food and drink for a healthy physical life. What's more, your presence at Mass is something God wants of you more than any other kind of thanksgiving or praise. Yes, morning and evening prayers are important. Yes, meal prayers are important. But more important than any of these is your prayerful participation in the Eucharist.

The word *Eucharist* means "thanksgiving" in Greek. When you attend Mass, you show your thanks to God for every good thing you enjoy in life. Neglecting to attend Sunday Mass is like taking all the good things your parents give you—food, shelter, clothes, education, health care, holiday gifts—and not once telling them "Thank you." We also celebrate the Eucharist because Christ told us to keep his memory alive in this way. Every Eucharist is a remembrance of the Death and Resurrection of Jesus.

The Sacrament of the Eucharist always includes: (1) the reading aloud of Scripture, (2) prayers of thanks to God the Father for the gift of his Son, Jesus, (3) the consecration of the bread and wine into the Body and Blood of Christ, and (4) the receiving of Christ's Body and Blood.

Just as water is needed for Baptism and Sacred Chrism is needed for Confirmation, two things are needed for Eucharist. They are bread made from wheat and wine made from grapes. Just as Baptism and Confirmation Rites include special words, so does the Eucharist. The words used by the priest to consecrate the bread and wine are the same words Jesus spoke the night before he died: "This is my Body, which will be given up for you. ... This is the chalice of my Blood."

Only a priest or bishop can consecrate the bread and wine for the Eucharist. Through the ministry of the priest, the Holy Spirit comes upon the bread and wine to change them into the Body and Blood of Christ.

FAQ Questions Parents Ask about First Eucharist

When you realize that this great sacrament makes you one with Christ, body and soul, you can see why the Eucharist is meant only for those who are free of serious sin. No one in a state of mortal sin should receive the Eucharist without first seeking God's forgiveness through the Sacrament of Penance. Less serious sins, however, are forgiven by the very act of receiving the Eucharist, a fact which just goes to show how much God wants to be with you!

That's how it is with Christ, too. Receiving the Eucharist can help you grow closer to him. Receiving this sacrament also brings you closer to everyone in his family, the Church. Think about it: What greater experience can you share with other human beings than together hearing God's Word, speaking with God, and dining at God's table?

Q How will my child benefit from using the *Invited by Christ* program?

A Jesus expresses the aim of the program—to draw your child into fuller and more active participation in the life of the Church. This means both in its life at Sunday worship and in the daily call to love one another.

Like every Catholic, your child will become one with Christ by receiving his Body and Blood. Eucharist is the sacrament that both nourishes the individual and creates the community that is the Body of Christ in the world—the Church. The effect of Eucharist is communion—the gift or grace of sharing God's life.

Invited by Christ will make your child aware of important events in Jesus' life, the main parts of the Mass, the Real Presence of Jesus in the Eucharist, and the way that receiving the Eucharist unites ourselves to Christ and to the Church family.

First Eucharist preparation aims to help children begin participating in the Eucharist. All of us deepen our understanding of the Eucharist and our response to its meaning through taking part in the sacrament over time. The Church asks us to gather and celebrate the Eucharist weekly so the sacrament can continuously nourish our growth as individuals and as members of the Church.

Q Why is the Eucharist so important for Catholics?

A There is no other sacrament quite like the Eucharist. The *Catechism* calls it "the heart and the summit of the Church's life" (*CCC*, 1407). The Eucharist is the heart because it is at the center of the Church's life. It is the summit because it is higher than any other form of worship or prayer. Eucharist gives us our identity as Church. We who share the Body and Blood of Christ are to become the Body of Christ, the Church. We who drink the cup pledge the pouring out of our lives as Jesus poured out his.

Q What help does *Invited by Christ* give me, as a parent?

A First of all, the program gives you background in this parent appendix. Second, this book includes a "With My Family" section at the end of each stepage Parents and their children can do these activities together as part of the child's preparation.

Q Whose job is it to prepare children for their First Eucharist?

A Both the family and the parish have important roles in preparing children for First Eucharist. From their child's birth, parents share their faith, first by choosing Baptism for their child and then by word and by example in everyday life. The *General Directory for Catechesis* tells us that the witness of parents' Christian life is irreplaceable in children's religious awakening (#226). The Second Vatican Council recognized the family as the center of living faith when it called the family the domestic Church.

When children reach the age of reason, the parish community, in the name of the whole Church, invites children to come to Jesus' table. In some parishes, parents act as catechists and prepare their own children to receive First

Eucharist. Some parishes offer a home-based religious education program as an option that parents may choose.

Most parishes train catechists to specialize in helping young children understand the Eucharist at their own level. But even in this situation, parish directors of faith formation realize that while catechists can teach children Gospel stories to help them understand Mass as Jesus' special meal and can explain the actions of the priest at Mass, they cannot take the place of parents and family. All members of the family—father, mother, other children, and members of the extended family—nurture the faith of children by receiving the sacraments, by praying, and by striving to live holy lives of sacrifice and charity.

Q What can I do as a parent to help?

A Only parents can help prepare their children for First Eucharist by taking them to Sunday Mass. Children learn by doing. Taking your children to Mass is an irreplaceable way parents nurture their children's Catholic faith.

Many children make their First Communions because grandparents insist or parents don't want them to miss out. But because of family circumstances, some of these children can't make their second, third, and fourth Communions, which are just as important as their first. Eucharist is the food and fuel of Christian life. Many catechists report that the first communicants they prepare don't or can't receive Holy Communion again in the next year.

It confuses children to have their catechists tell them they should go to Mass every Sunday and receive Holy Communion but then not be able to get there. Many parents with young children work long hours at more than one job. Weekend work schedules may make getting to church difficult. However, during your child's First Eucharist preparation year, it is vital to find ways to participate in Eucharist together.

The First Communion of an oldest child catches some parents with their commitment to participating in parish life a bit unsettled. During the young-adult years, many young people take a break from going to church or being active Catholics. A child's First Eucharist preparation can be a call to take one's own faith issues off the shelf, examine them, bring them up to date, and assess what one really wants for one's child.

Sharing the life of a parish community can be a real support and source of sustaining friendships for young parents, especially those whose own parents live at a distance. Worshiping with others tells children their parents share values and traditions with a wide variety of people.

Another reason to take your children to Mass is that the liturgy itself is a great teacher for young children. The sights, songs, signs, colors, smells, touches, and tastes of the Mass are all concrete and within the grasp of children.

Children will not remember all the words they hear, but they are likely to remember the people they watch each Sunday going to Holy Communion, the scenes they see in stained-glass windows, the incense wafting overhead.

Many catechists complain they can't teach much in the few hours of First Eucharist preparation or even in the weekly classes during the year. Catechists do only part of the work of nurturing and forming children's faith. Sharing the life of the community that prays together and does the work of justice together also instructs. This is the Catholic way to grow into a sacrament—through participation.

Celebrating the liturgical seasons in small ways at home through family rituals can help children realize the Sunday Gospels tell the story of Jesus' life. These celebrations can include:

- **Advent wreath and prayers**
- **Putting up the Nativity scene**
- **Keeping a palm branch**
- **Displaying a crucifix**
- **Reading Bible stories**
- **Celebrating baptismal anniversaries**
- **Baking a cake on Pentecost to celebrate the birthday of the Church**
- **Looking and talking about parents' wedding photos**
- **Talking about family members' Baptism and First Eucharist photos**

FAQ Questions Parents Ask about First Eucharist

Q What can my child really understand about the Eucharist?

A In preparing children for First Eucharist, we have to consider the concreteness of their thinking and their ability to understand symbols. We want to share our faith that the consecrated bread and wine are the Body and Blood of Christ. The guidelines in the *National Directory for Catechesis*, Chapter 5, #36, page 127, direct us to help children understand that this consecrated bread is different from any other bread. However, the children don't observe any concrete change in the bread.

The best approach to helping children begin to understand that they receive the Body of Christ in Holy Communion is to teach them about the Church, the People of God, who gather around the Risen Jesus. The children can experience Eucharist as a celebration of believers who remember that Jesus died and rose, as a meal shared by friends and started by Jesus before he died, and as the sacrament through which Jesus comes to us and shares with us his new life.

Primary children can only begin to understand that they receive the Body and Blood of Christ in First Eucharist. They must continue to share the faith of their parents and catechists. First Eucharist is a celebration of the shared faith of the parish community—young and old, parent and catechist—sharing and becoming the Body of Christ, the Church.

Q Does my child have to go to First Reconciliation before celebrating First Eucharist?

A Yes. The Church requires that your child celebrate the Sacrament of Reconciliation before receiving First Eucharist. A child must be free from mortal sin and in the state of grace to receive the Eucharist.

However, the preparation for and the celebration of the Sacrament of Reconciliation are usually separated by a significant time period from the preparation for First Eucharist and its celebration so that children do not receive the impression that they must always celebrate Reconciliation before receiving Holy Communion.

Q How will I know when my child is ready to receive First Eucharist?

A Talking with children is the main way to help discern their readiness to receive First Eucharist. Parents, catechists, and pastors share the responsibility of determining a child's readiness.

A child's desire to receive First Eucharist is important. Desire may arise from wanting to do what classmates are doing. This is fine. Companions can be good influences on children. Desire may arise from a child's own faith, which is beginning to form apart from the faith he or she shares with parents.

To receive First Eucharist, the Church requires only that a child be able to distinguish that the Body and Blood of Christ are different from the regular bread and drink we serve on our meal tables. Usually children must have reached the age of reason to make this distinction. They must affirm that Eucharist is the Body and Blood of Christ really present with us. A child must also be free from mortal sin and in the state of grace.

The Church does not require that children have a profound doctrinal understanding of the Eucharist. Rather, we invite children to join the community at Jesus' table and to learn the meaning of Eucharist through participating in the sacrament.

Joining the parish community to give thanks and praise through, with, and in Jesus' name and to receive Holy Communion with other Catholics will nurture both children's understanding of the sacramental action and their commitment to becoming the Body of Christ in the world, the Church.

Q What if my child doesn't want to receive First Eucharist?

A Parents and sponsors of children preparing for First Eucharist must allow for the unique development of every child. Eucharist is one of the three sacraments in the journey every Catholic makes on the way to becoming a full member of the Church. If a child does not want to receive First Eucharist, parents and catechists must pay attention to the child's feelings.

Perhaps the child has a misunderstanding that needs to be talked through. Perhaps a child simply isn't ready. If a child is eager to receive First Eucharist, parents and catechists should affirm his or her faith and desire. If not, parents need to help the child work his or her feelings through and seek the help of a catechist if they wish.

Q What are the rules regarding fasting before receiving the Eucharist?

A Church law requires Catholics to fast from food and beverage, with the exception of medicine and water, for one hour before Holy Communion.

Q What should my child wear for First Communion?

A White clothes are not a must, but they are a continuing custom in many parishes. Some directors of faith formation urge parents to play down the white dress and veil and the white shirt and tie because children at this age tend to remember these concrete aspects of the day much more than its central meaning.

Sometimes a child doesn't want to wear white, prefers another color, or wants to wear a favorite outfit. This is fine, but to enhance First Eucharist as a celebration, children should wear dress-up clothes.

Q Should my child drink from the Communion cup?

A In some parishes, children receive both the Body and Blood of Christ on their First Eucharist day. The Church encourages the use of both species, especially on important occasions, but we share fully in the Sacrament of the Eucharist whether we receive Holy Communion under both species or one species alone.

Sharing the cup is reasonably safe. Extraordinary Ministers of Holy Communion wipe the cup each time someone drinks.

Q What's the right way to receive Holy Communion?

A Children can receive Holy Communion in the hand or on the tongue. See page 74-75 for detailed instructions on how to practice receiving Communion through both options.

Q What if my spouse isn't Catholic?

A Discuss with your pastor and director of religious education how your parish handles interfaith matters. Your parish will probably want you to invite your spouse to be as full a part of your child's First Eucharist as possible.

If your spouse is not comfortable taking part in the First Eucharist celebration, consider having the child's grandparents, godparents, or family friends join in standing with the child on this important day.

Q Should our family have a celebration for our first communicant?

A A family celebration will add importance to the day. Do what is customary for your family. Invite family and friends or go out for a special meal. If you customarily give gifts, help family and friends know what gifts your child needs.

Treasures of the Catholic Faith: The Mass

The Mass

The Sunday celebration of the Eucharist, traditionally known as the Holy Sacrifice of the Mass, is at the heart of the Church's life.

Introductory Rites

- **Entrance Procession**–All stand and sing as the priest and ministers enter the church.
- **Sign of the Cross and Greeting**–The priest greets the people and they respond.
- **Rite of Blessing and Sprinkling of Holy Water**–Used on some Sundays, this rite reminds people of their Baptism.
- **Penitential Act**–On other Sundays, the people confess their sinfulness and the priest reminds them of God's forgiveness.
- **Gloria**–All praise God with this hymn.
- **Collect**–The priest invites people to offer prayers for their needs.

Liturgy of the Word

- **First Reading**–A reader, or lector, proclaims an Old Testament passage. It shows how Jesus fulfills the promise of the Old Testament.
- **Responsorial Psalm**–The people respond to the First Reading with a psalm. It is best for the Responsorial Psalm to be sung.
- **Second Reading**–A lector, or reader, proclaims a passage from the New Testament.
- **Alleluia/Gospel Acclamation**–All stand and sing praise to Jesus.
- **Gospel Reading**–The people stand and listen to a story about Jesus.
- **Homily**–The priest explains the day's readings. He shows how God is alive and active in the world today.
- **Profession of Faith**–All stand and profess their faith by proclaiming the Nicene Creed or the Apostles' Creed.
- **Prayer of the Faithful**–The people pray for their needs and the needs of the Church, community, and world.

Liturgy of the Eucharist

- **Preparation of the Altar and Collection and Procession with Gifts**–The servers prepare the altar, and members of the assembly bring up the gifts of bread, wine, and donated money.
- **Prayer Over the Offerings**–The priest prays that the gifts may be acceptable to God.
- **Eucharistic Prayer**–During this prayer, the bread and wine become the Body and Blood of Christ. This happens through the ministry of the priest through the power of the Holy Spirit.
- **Preface Acclamation or Holy, Holy, Holy**–The people sing the prayer of the angels found in Isaiah 6:3.
- **Memorial Acclamation of the Mystery of Faith**–The people proclaim the mystery of their faith: through his Death and Resurrection, Christ has set us free.
- **Great Amen**–By saying "Amen," the people express belief that Jesus is in their midst.

Communion Rite

- **Our Father**–The people pray in the words Jesus gave them.
- **Rite of Peace**–All share a sign of peace to show their unity in Christ.
- **The Breaking, or Fraction, with the Lamb of God**–The people recognize Jesus as the Lamb of God, who takes away the sins of the world.
- **Communion Song**–The people sing as they come forward for Communion.
- **Communion**–The people receive the Body and Blood of Christ.
- **Period of Silence or Song of Praise**–The people reflect on the presence of the Lord within and among them.
- **Prayer after Communion**–The people pray that their Communion will help them make a difference in the world.

Concluding Rites

- **Blessing**–The priest blesses the people in the name of the Father, Son, and Holy Spirit.
- **Dismissal**–The people are reminded of their mission to love and serve the Lord.

Hail Mary

Hail Mary, full of grace,
the Lord is with thee!
Blessed art thou among women,
and blessed is the fruit of thy womb, Jesus.
Holy Mary, Mother of God,
pray for us sinners,
now and at the hour of our death.
Amen.

Sign of the Cross

In the name of the Father,
and of the Son,
and of the Holy Spirit.
Amen.

The Lord's Prayer (Our Father)

Our Father, who art in heaven,
hallowed be thy name;
thy kingdom come,
thy will be done on earth as it is in heaven.
Give us this day our daily bread,
and forgive us our trespasses
as we forgive those who trespass against us;
and lead us not into temptation,
but deliver us from evil.
Amen.

Glory Be to the Father

Glory be to the Father,
and to the Son,
and to the Holy Spirit.
As it was in the beginning,
is now, and ever shall be,
world without end.
Amen.

Prayer to Jesus Christ in the Eucharist

Lord Jesus, I believe that you are truly present in the Eucharist.

As I receive you in Holy Communion,
help me to love as you loved,
serve as you served, so I can be the
Body of Christ to others.
Amen.

A Prayer on the Day of My First Holy Communion

Dear Jesus, thank you for coming to me for the very first time in the Eucharist.

Help me remember that the Bread is really your Body and that the chalice holds your Blood, under the appearances of ordinary bread and wine.

As you become part of me, may I
become more like you.
In your name, Lord Jesus. Amen.

My Prayer to Jesus

(Write your own prayer here.)

....

....

....

....

....

Act of Contrition Prayers

O my God,
I am sorry and repent with all my heart
for all the wrong I have done
and for the good I have failed to do,
because by sinning I have offended you,
who are all good and worthy to be loved above all things.
I firmly resolve, with the help of your grace,
to do penance,
to sin no more,
and to avoid the occasions of sin.
Through the merits of the Passion of our Savior Jesus Christ,
Lord, have mercy.
Amen.
(Order of Penance)

Father, I am sorry for all the bad I have done,
and the good I have failed to do.
I will sincerely try to do better,
especially . . . [here mention a particular resolution]
and to walk in your light.
Amen.

Lord Jesus, Son of God,
have mercy on me, a sinner.
Amen.

My God,
I am sorry for my sins with all my heart.
In choosing to do wrong
and in failing to do good,
I have sinned against you
whom I should love above all things.
I firmly intend, with your help,
to do penance,
to sin no more,
and to avoid whatever leads me to sin.
Our Savior Jesus Christ
suffered and died for us.
In his name, my God, have mercy.
Amen.

Recommended Songs from Composer John Burland

Belonging Through Baptism
Sign of the Cross
Jesus This Day Gather Us
Go Now and Listen to God's Word
Come Back
Reconcile
Act of Contrition
My Peace Be with You Always
Lord Bless Me on This Day
Father Today

O Lord, We Come to You
Through This Gift of Love
Receive this Gift of Love
Now Go

"He who sings prays twice."
-Saint Augustine

Get your parent's permission and check out the *Invited by Christ* coordinating music playlist, which features songs for your sacramental journey (written by well-known Catholic composer John Burland)!

How to Receive the Sacrament of Reconciliation

Examination of Conscience

I love God and want to follow God's ways. I am sorry for my sins.

Confession

I confess my sins. I tell the priest any ways I have failed to keep God's commandments. I tell the priest about my unloving actions.

Penance

The priest gives me a penance. A penance is often a prayer to pray or a loving action to do. This is a way to make up for ways my actions have hurt or harmed someone. I pray an Act of Contrition.

Absolution

The priest absolves my sins in Jesus' name. He shows me that God forgives me.

(See page 31 for detailed step-by-step instructions.)

How to Receive the Eucharist

Before joining the Communion procession, pray an Act of Contrition.

When you are about to receive Communion, bow your head as a gesture of reverence.

To receive the Body of Christ in your hands: put your left hand in the palm of your right hand, palms up (or right hand in the palm of your left hand, if you are left-handed). The priest, deacon, or extraordinary minister of Holy Communion will say, "The Body of Christ." You respond, "Amen." The Body of Christ will be placed in your hand. Pick up the Host with your other hand and put it on your tongue. Close your mouth and swallow.

To receive the Body of Christ on your tongue: The priest, deacon, or extraordinary minister of Holy Communion will say, "The Body of Christ." You respond, "Amen." Then open your mouth and put your tongue out. The priest or minister will put the Body of Christ on your tongue. Close your mouth and swallow.

To receive the Blood of Christ, the priest, deacon, or extraordinary minister of Holy Communion will say, "The Blood of Christ." You respond, "Amen." The priest or minister will give you the chalice. Take it and drink a sip from it. Then hand the chalice back.

Return to your place and sing the Communion song. Then pray a thank you prayer in your own words for Jesus coming to you in Holy Communion.

Autographs

MEMORIES FROM MY FIRST HOLY COMMUNION

These are the people who shared this special day with me.

Paste a photo from your First Holy Communion and/or invite family and friends to write a special note.